U.S.A. TRAVEL GUIDES

NEW YORK

BY ANN HEINRICHS • ILLUSTRATED BY MATT KANIA

The Child's World®
childsworld.com

Published by The Child's World®
1980 Lookout Drive • Mankato, MN 56003-1705
800-599-READ • www.childsworld.com

Photo Credits
Photographs ©: Joshua Haviv/Shutterstock Images,
cover, 1; Songquan Deng/Shutterstock Images, 7;
Colin D. Young/Shutterstock Images, 8; Michael Rega/
Shutterstock Images, 11; Eden, Janine and Jim CC2.0, 12;
iStockphoto, 15, 20; Joseph Sohm/Shutterstock Images,
16; Sean Donohue Photo/Shutterstock Images, 19;
Svetlana Borisova/Shutterstock Images, 23; Brian Holland
CC2.0, 25; A. G. Photos/Shutterstock Images, 27; Samuel
Borges Photography/Shutterstock Images, 28; Felix
Lipov/Shutterstock Images, 31, 32; Nagel Photography/
Shutterstock Images, 35; Shutterstock Images, 37 (top),
37 (bottom)

ISBN 9781503819726
LCCN 2016961184

Printing
Printed in the United States of America
PA02334

Ann Heinrichs is the author of more than 100 books for children and young adults. She has also enjoyed successful careers as a children's book editor and an advertising copywriter. Ann grew up in Fort Smith, Arkansas, and lives in Chicago, Illinois.

About the Author
Ann Heinrichs

Matt Kania loves maps and, as a kid, dreamed of making them. In school he studied geography and cartography, and today he makes maps for a living. Matt's favorite thing about drawing maps is learning about the places they represent. Many of the maps he has created can be found in books, magazines, videos, Web sites, and public places.

About the
Map Illustrator
Matt Kania

On the cover: The skyline of New York City.

OUR NEW YORK TRIP

NEW YORK

Ready for a tour of the Empire State? That's New York! Now, New York City is pretty famous. But New York State is really great!

Take this trip, and you'll stand beneath thundering waterfalls. You'll spin thread and blow glass. You'll ride a ship. You'll roam among foxes and deer. You'll see the Statue of Liberty. And you'll watch the Headless Horseman riding by!

Does that sound like a fun tour? Then buckle your seat belt. We're on our way!

WELCOME TO
NEW YORK

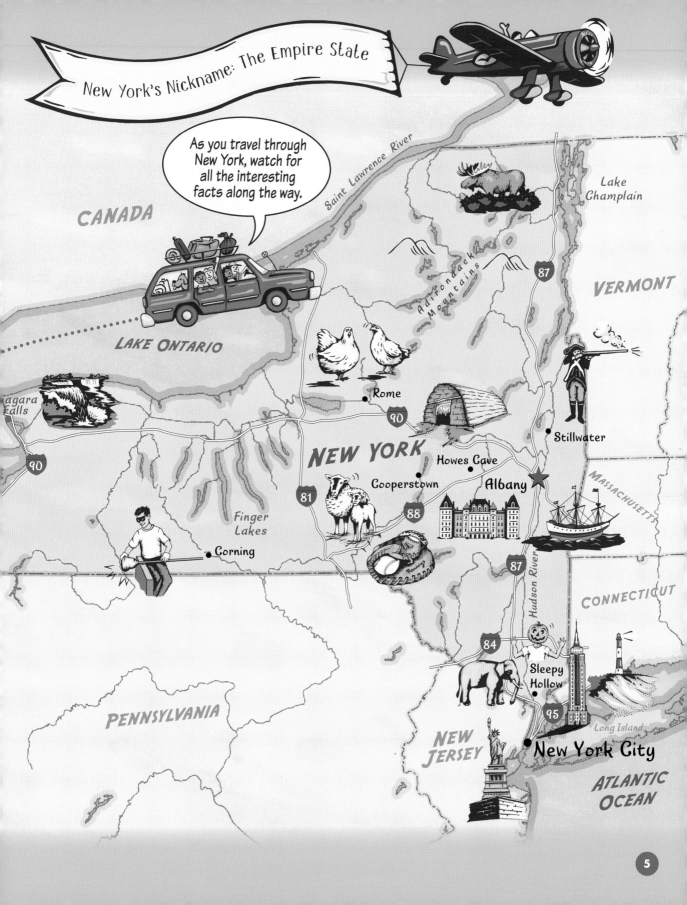

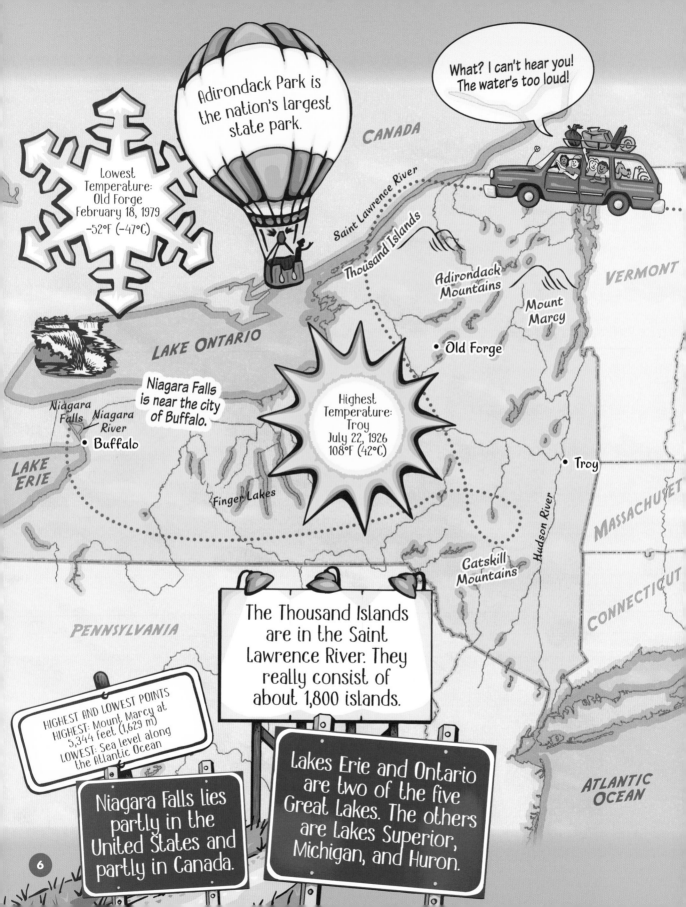

GETTING CLOSE TO NIAGARA FALLS

Put on your poncho. Then follow the guide. Soon you're right at the base of Niagara Falls. The water crashes in a thundering roar!

Niagara Falls is a waterfall on the Niagara River. This river connects Lake Erie and Lake Ontario. Lake Ontario flows into the Saint Lawrence River. This river eventually empties into the Atlantic Ocean. The Hudson River reaches the Atlantic, too. It flows down the state from north to south.

The Adirondack Mountains rise in the northeast. Farther south are the Catskill Mountains. Many lakes are scattered through the state. The Finger Lakes are long and thin— like fingers!

Tour boats will take visitors close to Niagara Falls.

Walk softly through the Adirondack Mountains. You'll hear lots of animal sounds. Chipmunks and squirrels are chirping. Frogs and toads are croaking. A loud, high-pitched noise may startle you. It sounds like really crazy laughing. That's a waterbird called a loon.

Deer and moose live in the Adirondack forests. Lots of beavers live there, too. They build homes along the water. The homes look like big mounds of sticks.

Black bears and bobcats lurk in the forest. You may not see them, though. They're very shy!

The Hudson River flows through the Adirondack Mountains.

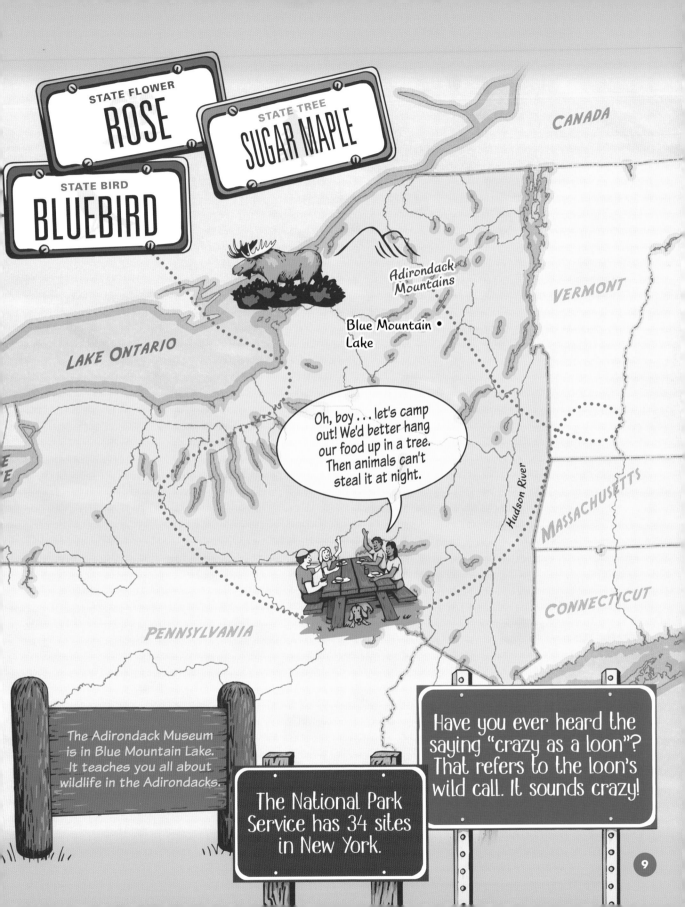

STATE FLOWER
ROSE

STATE TREE
SUGAR MAPLE

STATE BIRD
BLUEBIRD

CANADA

Adirondack Mountains

VERMONT

Blue Mountain • Lake

LAKE ONTARIO

Oh, boy . . . let's camp out! We'd better hang our food up in a tree. Then animals can't steal it at night.

Hudson River

MASSACHUSETTS

CONNECTICUT

PENNSYLVANIA

The Adirondack Museum is in Blue Mountain Lake. It teaches you all about wildlife in the Adirondacks.

The National Park Service has 34 sites in New York.

Have you ever heard the saying "crazy as a loon"? That refers to the loon's wild call. It sounds crazy!

9

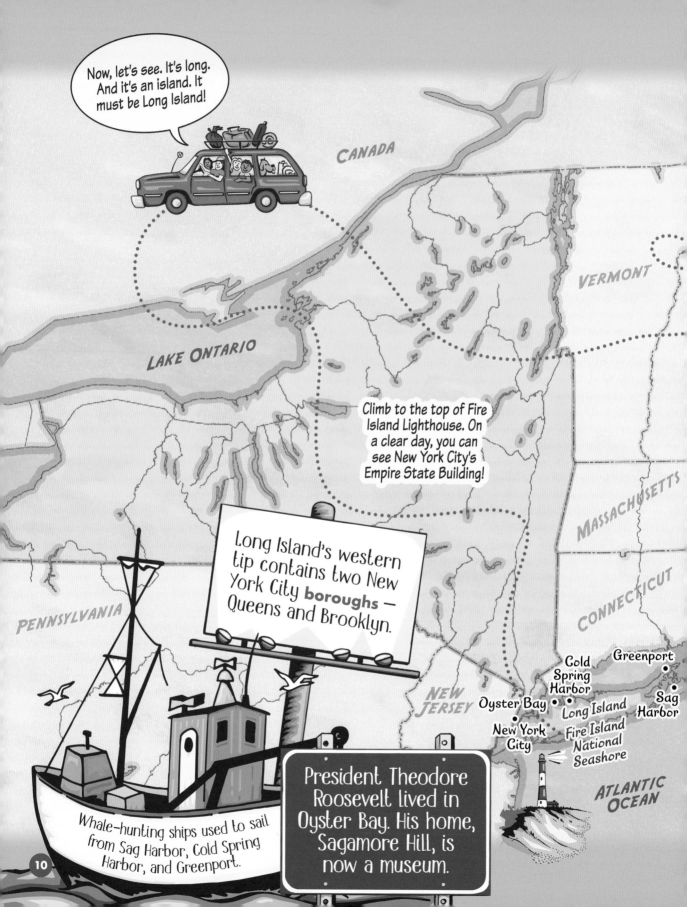

Now, let's see. It's long. And it's an island. It must be Long Island!

CANADA

VERMONT

LAKE ONTARIO

Climb to the top of Fire Island Lighthouse. On a clear day, you can see New York City's Empire State Building!

MASSACHUSETTS

Long Island's western tip contains two New York City **boroughs** — Queens and Brooklyn.

CONNECTICUT

PENNSYLVANIA

Cold Spring Harbor • • Greenport

NEW JERSEY

Oyster Bay • • Long Island • • Sag Harbor

New York City • Fire Island National Seashore

Whale-hunting ships used to sail from Sag Harbor, Cold Spring Harbor, and Greenport.

President Theodore Roosevelt lived in Oyster Bay. His home, Sagamore Hill, is now a museum.

ATLANTIC OCEAN

LONG ISLAND'S FIRE ISLAND NATIONAL SEASHORE

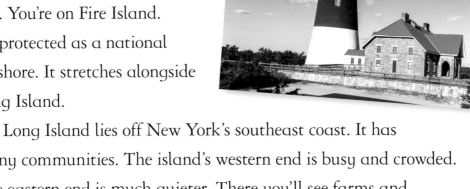

Climb the high sand dunes. Watch the ocean from a sandy beach. Roam through forests where deer and foxes live. You're on Fire Island. It's protected as a national seashore. It stretches alongside Long Island.

Long Island lies off New York's southeast coast. It has many communities. The island's western end is busy and crowded. The eastern end is much quieter. There you'll see farms and fishing villages.

Beaches stretch along much of the south shore. The north shore was once called the Gold Coast. Many rich people built summer homes there. Some of those homes are now museums.

Learn about lighthouse keepers at the Fire Island Lighthouse.

Make a doll out of corn **husks**. Pound corn into cornmeal. Examine Native American art and tools.

You're visiting the Iroquois Indian Museum in Howes Cave. There you will learn about the Iroquois way of life. You can even watch **traditional** Iroquois dancing and listen to stories.

The Iroquois is a group of five tribes including the Mohawk, Seneca, Oneida, Cayuga, and Onondaga. They have lived in New York since before Europeans arrived. Historically, Iroquois built longhouses as homes. They raised corn, beans, and squash. The Iroquois respected the natural world. They hunted only for food. In the 1600s, their villages were located across what is now upstate New York.

Today, Iroquois Native Americans live in many communities across the United States and Canada, including New York.

A longhouse is a long, narrow building that the Iroquois built.

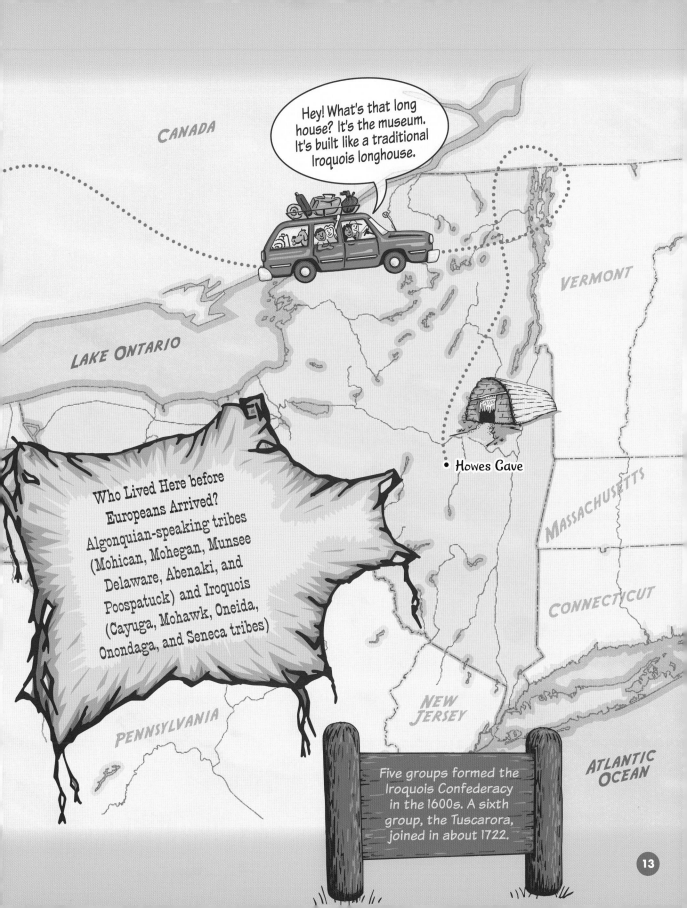

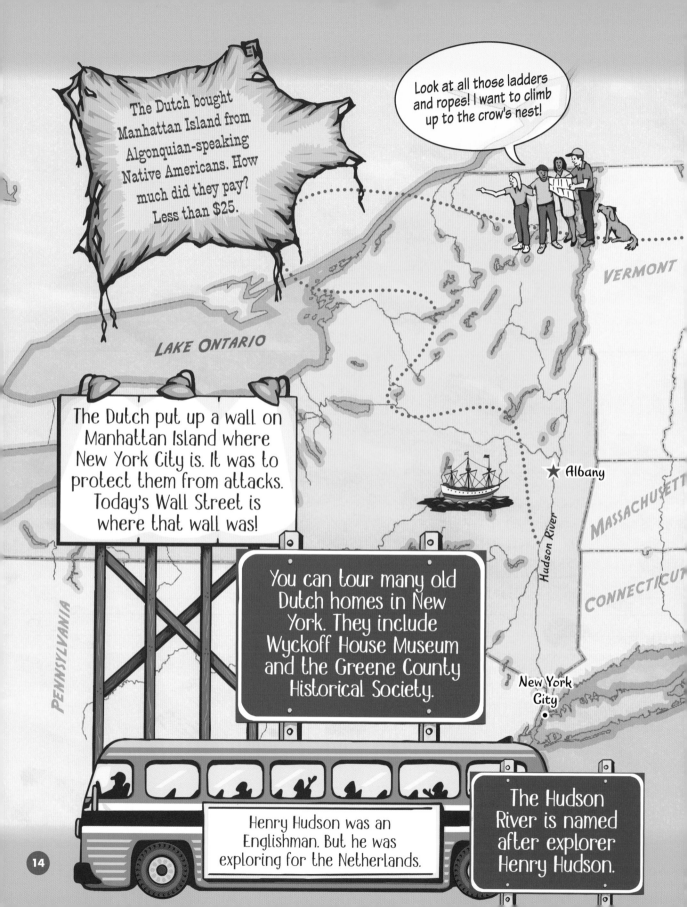

Climb aboard the ship. High atop the mast is the crow's nest. That's where sailors perched to see far away. Soon you're sailing down the Hudson River!

You're taking a tour on the *Half Moon*. It's built like Henry Hudson's ship the *Half Moon*. Hudson sailed to present-day New York in 1609. He claimed it for the Netherlands. This new land was named New Netherland.

Many **Dutch** settlers soon moved in. They founded Fort Orange in 1624. It became Albany. They also founded New Amsterdam. It's now New York City.

The English took over the region in 1664. They named it New York. It became one of the 13 English **colonies**.

Hop aboard the Half Moon *and explore the Hudson River!*

The state capitol in Albany is huge. It covers more ground than one football field! Inside, it's like a beautiful castle. Its tall columns reach up to high ceilings. You'll see stained glass windows and rich, dark wood. The state government offices are in this building.

All states have three branches of government. New York is no different. One branch makes the state laws. Another branch carries out those laws. It's headed by the governor. The third branch consists of judges. They listen to cases in court. Then they decide whether laws have been broken.

The capitol building was built in 1899. It cost more than $25 million to build!

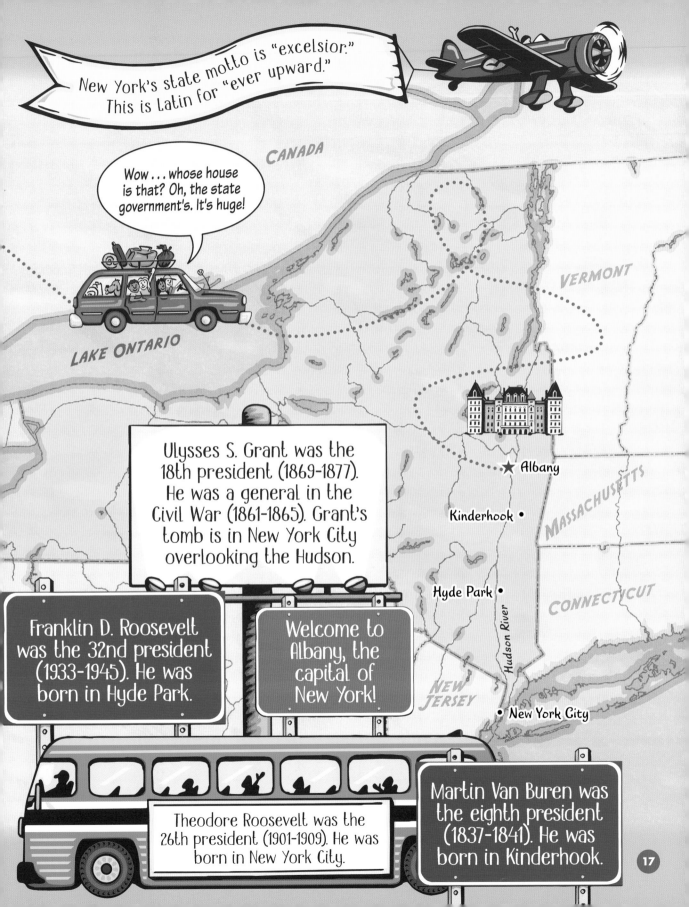

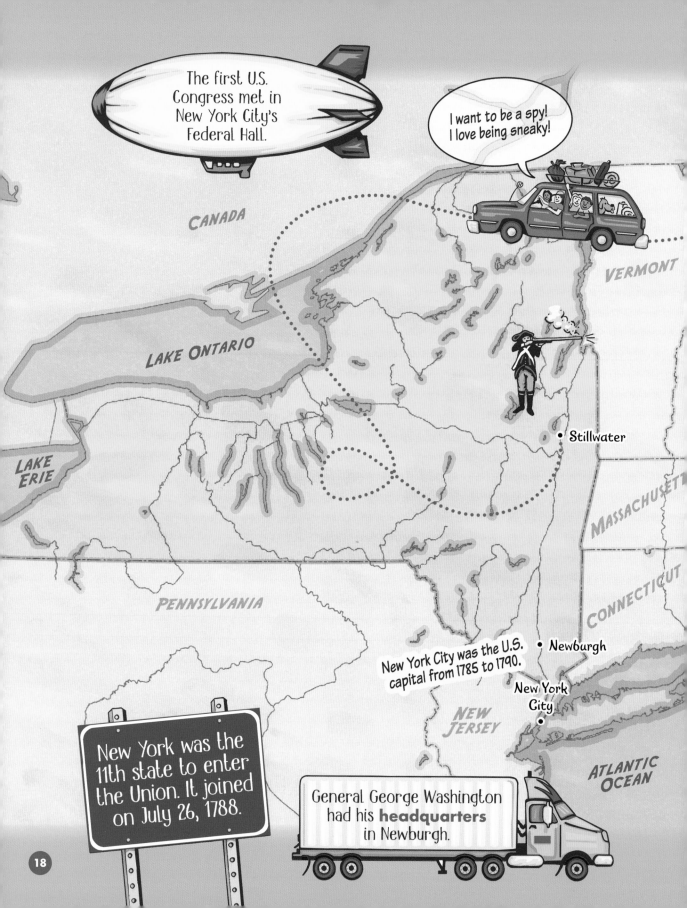

THE BATTLE OF SARATOGA AT STILLWATER

In the autumn of 1777, cannons boomed and **muskets** were fired on Saratoga Battlefield. British and American soldiers were fighting an important battle in the Revolutionary War (1775–1783). American colonists were fighting for freedom from Great Britain. They won! The 13 colonies became the first 13 states.

General George Washington led the colonial army. He became the first U.S. president. And New York City became the nation's capital!

Today, visitors of Saratoga National Historical Park in Stillwater can tour the battlefield. You can also stop by the visitor center and see artifacts and exhibits. There's lots of information here about the Battle of Saratoga.

Watch a war reenactment of the Battle of Saratoga.

Here's someone making a broom. There's someone hammering hot metal into tools. Others are carving wood or making candles. You can join in, too. Try your hand at spinning **flax** into thread.

You're enjoying a day at Village Crossroad. It's part of the Farmers' Museum Cooperstown. It shows how New York farmers once lived.

New York farmers are still busy today. Many of them raise dairy cattle. Dairy cows are good at producing milk. Milk is New York's leading farm product.

Other farmers grow fruits and vegetables. Do you like apples? Your next apple might come from New York. It's a top apple-growing state.

Learn how to make candles at the Farmers' Museum.

Only California and Wisconsin produce more milk than New York.

What Are New York's Fishing Products?
Oysters, clams, bluefish, striped bass, perch, trout, and salmon

CANADA

VERMONT

LAKE ONTARIO

The state fair is held in Syracuse from late August through early September each year.

Syracuse •

Hey ... let's pet those big, woolly sheep. See those red pigs? Look at those huge duck eggs!

• Cooperstown

MASSACHUSETTS

PENNSYLVANIA

CONNECTICUT

Only Washington State produces more apples than New York.

What Does New York Raise?
Milk and dairy products, cattle, and chickens

Only California and Washington State produce more grapes than New York.

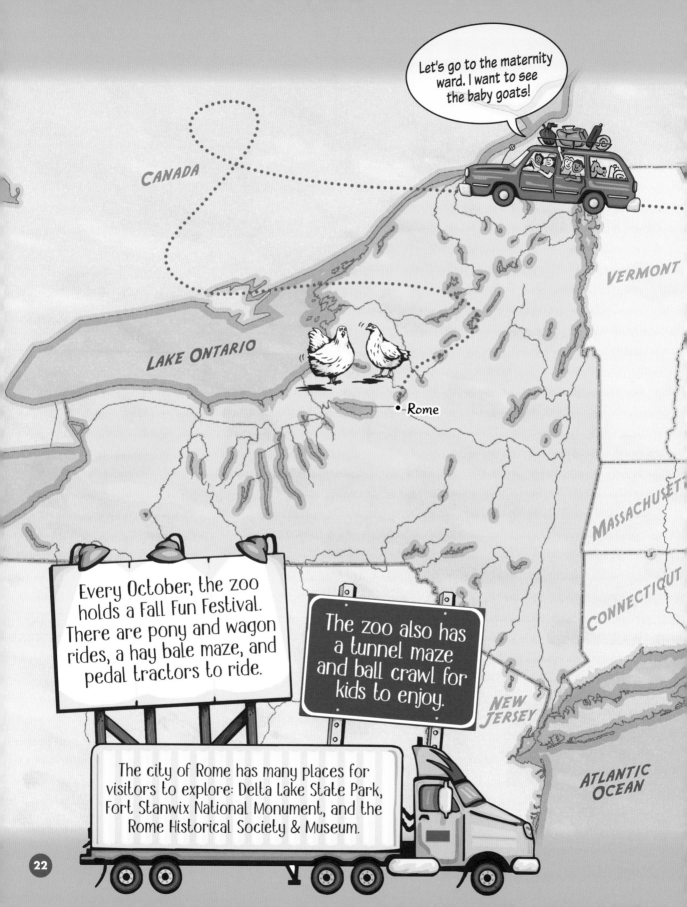

Let's go to the maternity ward. I want to see the baby goats!

CANADA

VERMONT

LAKE ONTARIO

• Rome

MASSACHUSETTS

CONNECTICUT

Every October, the zoo holds a Fall Fun Festival. There are pony and wagon rides, a hay bale maze, and pedal tractors to ride.

The zoo also has a tunnel maze and ball crawl for kids to enjoy.

NEW JERSEY

ATLANTIC OCEAN

The city of Rome has many places for visitors to explore: Delta Lake State Park, Fort Stanwix National Monument, and the Rome Historical Society & Museum.

FORT RICKEY'S ZOO IN ROME

Fort Rickey Children's Discovery Zoo in Rome is different from a typical zoo. Here, visitors can get up close and personal to the animals. Kids can even pet them!

The zoo has hands-on activities for kids of all ages. You will walk through exhibits of native and exotic animals. You can attend hands-on animal shows. You can even stop by the petting zoo and cuddle with baby goats!

Animals from all over the world call the zoo home. There are African snakes and lemurs, Australian birds, North American gray wolves, South American spider monkeys, and more.

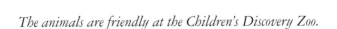

The animals are friendly at the Children's Discovery Zoo.

Watch the master glassblowers. They melt the glass until it's stretchy. They blow into a tube to add air. Then they pull and fold it into shapes. Presto! There's a glass fish!

You're watching the Hot Glass Demos. It happens at the Corning Museum of Glass. Its glassblowers make glass the old-fashioned way.

New Yorkers once made lots of things by hand. Today, factories do most of the work. New York's factories make medicines and machines. Others make parts for computers or cars. Food, clothes, chemical products, electronics, and books are New York products, too.

Glass blowing was invented thousands of years ago. The technique is still used today.

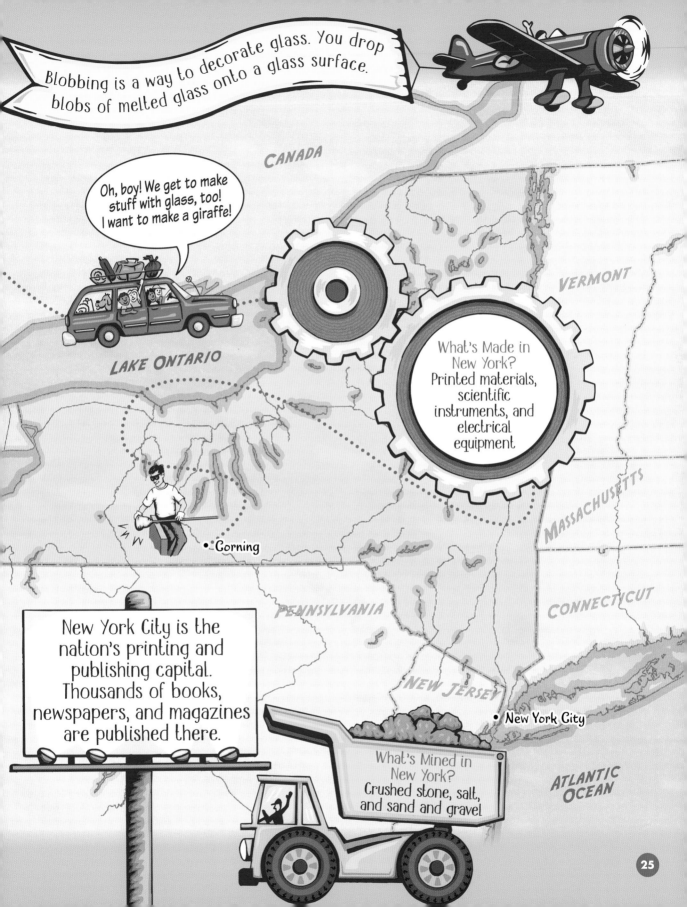

Blobbing is a way to decorate glass. You drop blobs of melted glass onto a glass surface.

Oh, boy! We get to make stuff with glass, too! I want to make a giraffe!

CANADA

VERMONT

LAKE ONTARIO

What's Made in New York?
Printed materials, scientific instruments, and electrical equipment

• Corning

MASSACHUSETTS

PENNSYLVANIA

CONNECTICUT

New York City is the nation's printing and publishing capital. Thousands of books, newspapers, and magazines are published there.

NEW JERSEY

• New York City

What's Mined in New York?
Crushed stone, salt, and sand and gravel

ATLANTIC OCEAN

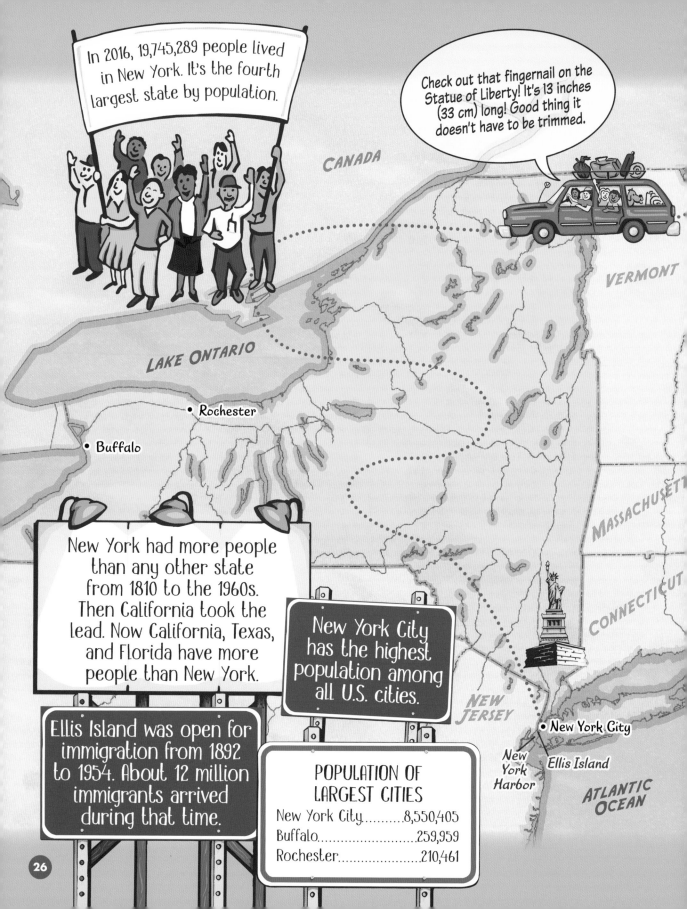

In 2016, 19,745,289 people lived in New York. It's the fourth largest state by population.

Check out that fingernail on the Statue of Liberty! It's 13 inches (33 cm) long! Good thing it doesn't have to be trimmed.

CANADA

VERMONT

LAKE ONTARIO

• Rochester

• Buffalo

MASSACHUSETTS

New York had more people than any other state from 1810 to the 1960s. Then California took the lead. Now California, Texas, and Florida have more people than New York.

New York City has the highest population among all U.S. cities.

CONNECTICUT

NEW JERSEY

• New York City

New York Harbor

Ellis Island

ATLANTIC OCEAN

Ellis Island was open for immigration from 1892 to 1954. About 12 million immigrants arrived during that time.

POPULATION OF LARGEST CITIES
New York City...........8,550,405
Buffalo..........................259,959
Rochester.....................210,461

THE STATUE OF LIBERTY IN NEW YORK HARBOR

There she stands in New York Harbor. She's the Statue of Liberty. Millions of **immigrants** saw her as they arrived. She's a sign of freedom in a new land.

Near the statue is Ellis Island. New immigrants used to register there. In the late 1800s, thousands of people arrived. Many settled right in New York City. Some immigrants had come from Italy, Ireland, or Germany. Others were from Poland or Russia.

Today, New Yorkers have roots in many countries. They come from Europe, Asia, and Africa. Many come from Spanish-speaking lands. There are also many Native Americans that live in New York. There are eight tribes in New York today. New Yorkers all have special foods, music, and customs. New York life would be boring without its **diverse** population!

The Statue of Liberty weighs 225 tons (204 metric tons).

Visit the Empire State Building in New York City. Take the elevators to the top. Walk around the deck and gaze out. You will see tall buildings everywhere. You may see rivers and mountains, too.

It's easy to imagine you're a king or queen. That helps you understand New York's nickname. It's called the Empire State. An empire is a huge kingdom.

New York grew to become a very important state. It's one of the top manufacturing states. It's also a leading center for music and art. Many TV networks and banks have their headquarters there.

New York became a world center, too. The United Nations was formed in 1945. It made New York City its home.

It took a little more than a year to build the Empire State Building.

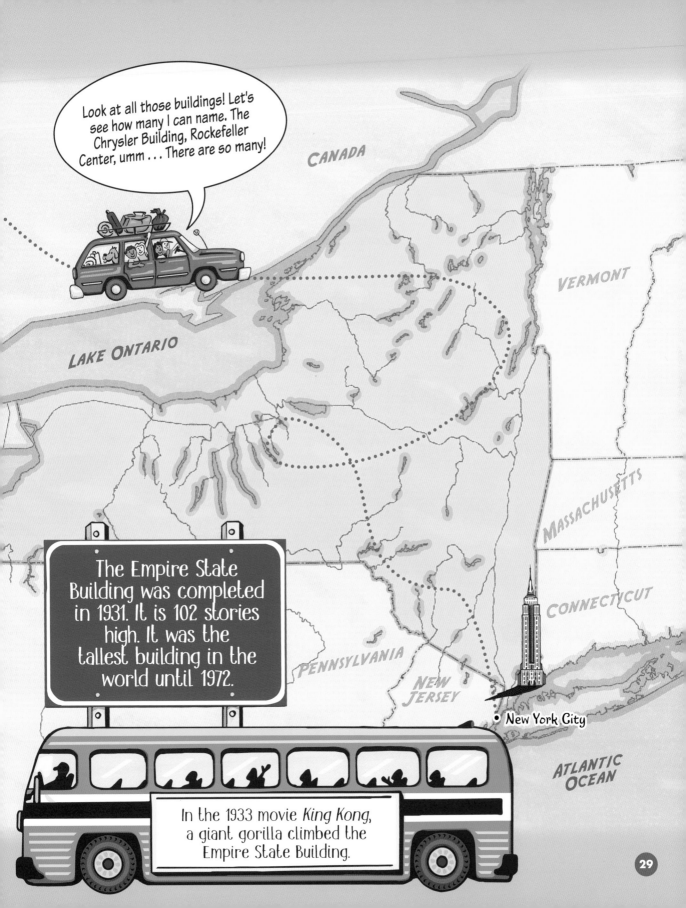

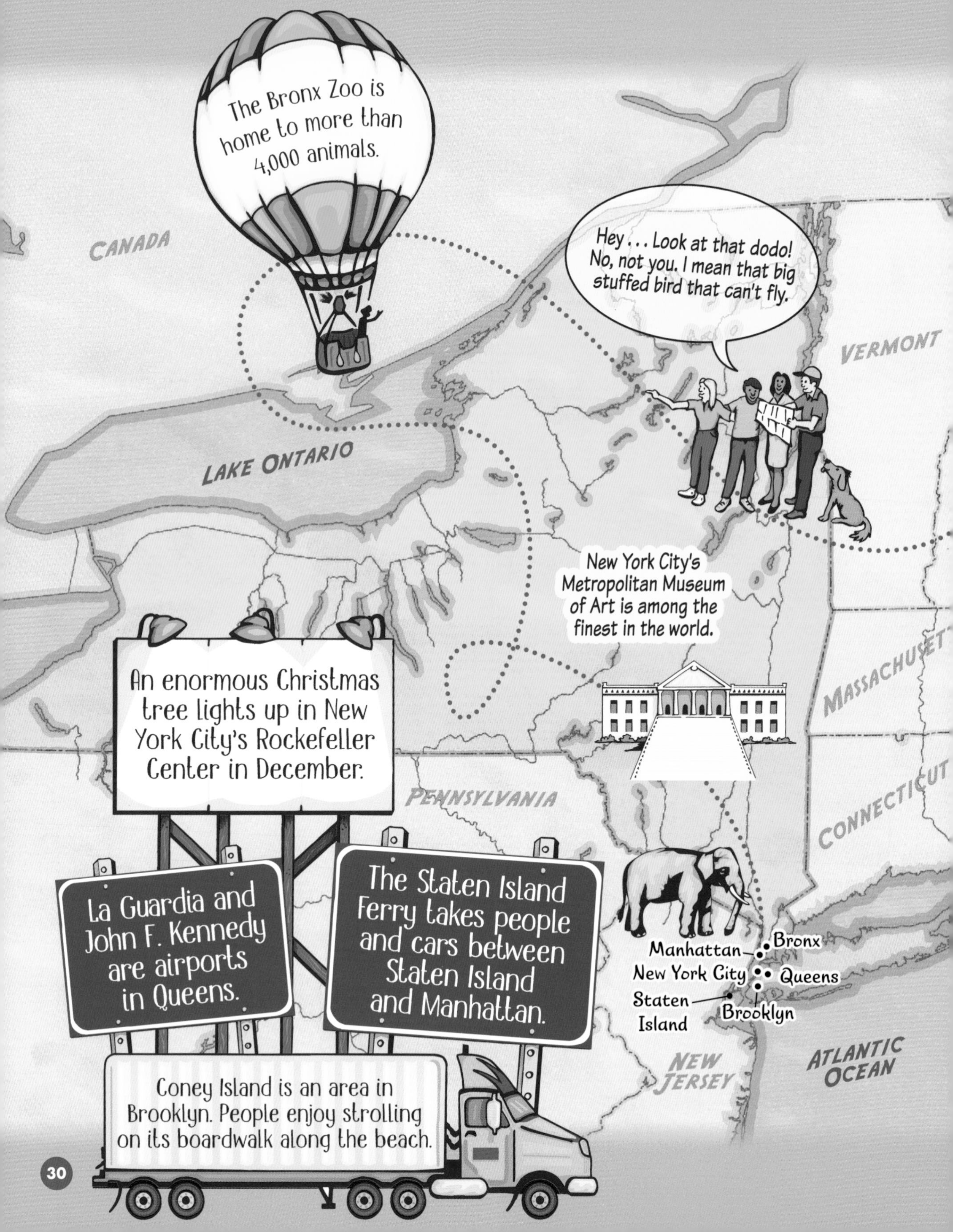
The Bronx Zoo is home to more than 4,000 animals.
CANADA
Hey . . . Look at that dodo! No, not you. I mean that big stuffed bird that can't fly.
VERMONT
LAKE ONTARIO
New York City's Metropolitan Museum of Art is among the finest in the world.
MASSACHUSETTS
An enormous Christmas tree lights up in New York City's Rockefeller Center in December.
PENNSYLVANIA
CONNECTICUT
La Guardia and John F. Kennedy are airports in Queens.
The Staten Island Ferry takes people and cars between Staten Island and Manhattan.
Bronx
Manhattan
New York City
Queens
Staten Island
Brooklyn
ATLANTIC OCEAN
NEW JERSEY
Coney Island is an area in Brooklyn. People enjoy strolling on its boardwalk along the beach.

MANHATTAN AND THE AMERICAN MUSEUM OF NATURAL HISTORY

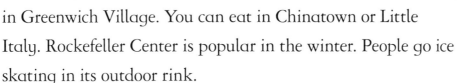

Explore the world of dinosaurs. Learn about ancient ways of healing. Find out how elephants live. You're at the American Museum of Natural History!

New York City has many cool places. You'll see plays and musicals on Broadway. You'll shop for funky clothes in Greenwich Village. You can eat in Chinatown or Little Italy. Rockefeller Center is popular in the winter. People go ice skating in its outdoor rink.

All these places are in Manhattan. Manhattan is just one of the city's boroughs. The others are Brooklyn, the Bronx, Queens, and Staten Island.

See dinosaur bones at the American Museum of Natural History.

HALLOWEEN IN SLEEPY HOLLOW

Ghosts and witches are roaming around. A storyteller is telling scary stories. Look—the Headless Horseman is riding by!

Don't worry. It's Halloween time at Philipsburg Manor. This old home is near Tarrytown. It's in an area called Sleepy Hollow.

The Headless Horseman lives only in storybooks. He appears in "The Legend of Sleepy Hollow." That's a spooky tale by Washington Irving.

Irving himself lived in the Sleepy Hollow area. People can visit his home, called Sunnyside. Scary things happen there on Halloween, too!

A jack-o'-lantern greets Sleepy Hollow visitors on Halloween.

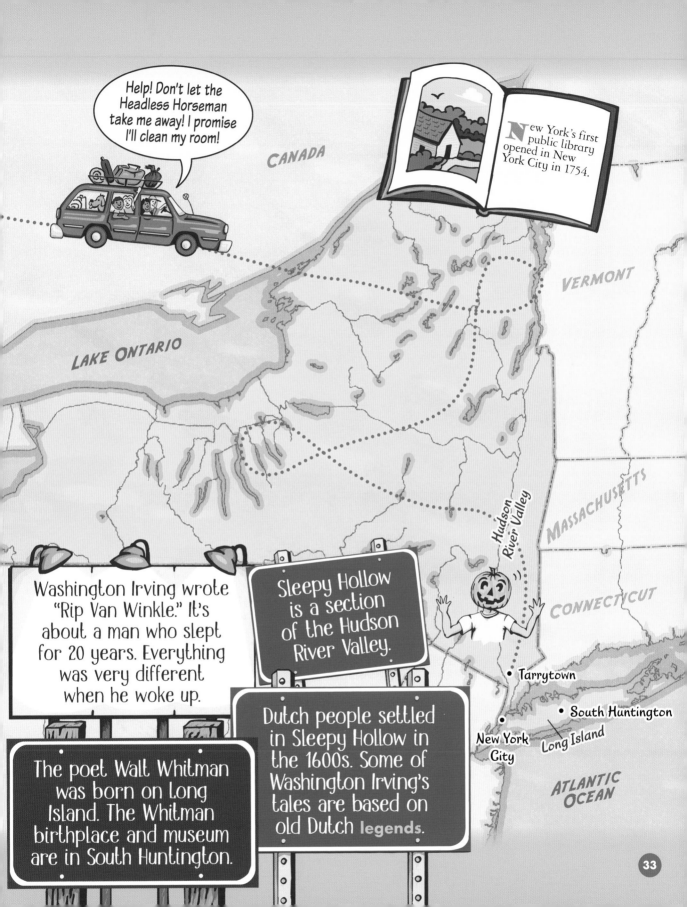

Help! Don't let the Headless Horseman take me away! I promise I'll clean my room!

New York's first public library opened in New York City in 1754.

CANADA

VERMONT

LAKE ONTARIO

Hudson River Valley

MASSACHUSETTS

CONNECTICUT

Washington Irving wrote "Rip Van Winkle." It's about a man who slept for 20 years. Everything was very different when he woke up.

Sleepy Hollow is a section of the Hudson River Valley.

• Tarrytown

• South Huntington

New York City

Long Island

Dutch people settled in Sleepy Hollow in the 1600s. Some of Washington Irving's tales are based on old Dutch legends.

The poet Walt Whitman was born on Long Island. The Whitman birthplace and museum are in South Huntington.

ATLANTIC OCEAN

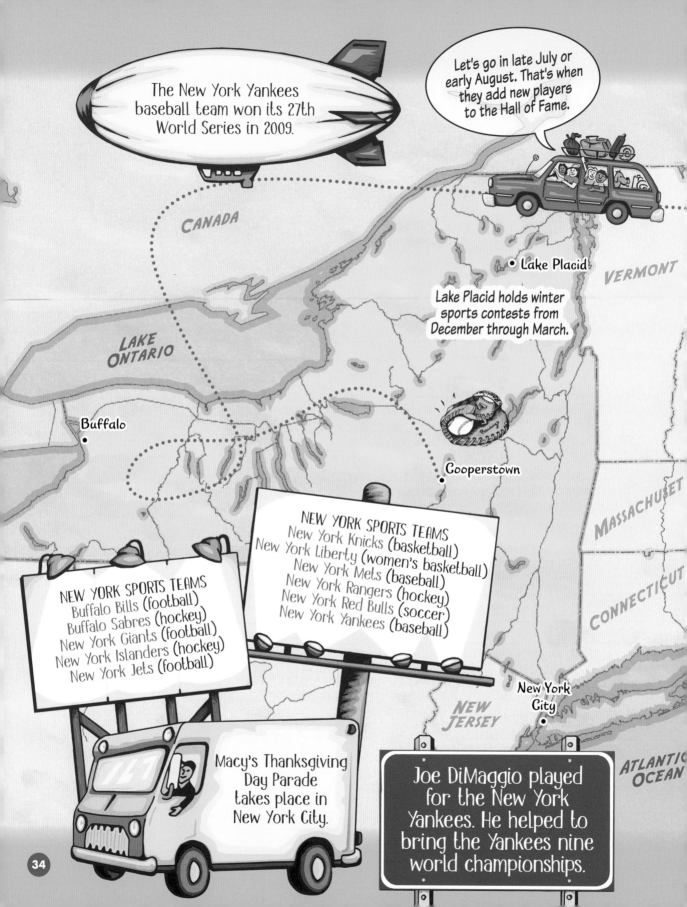

COOPERSTOWN'S BASEBALL HALL OF FAME

New York's Baseball Hall of Fame in Cooperstown honors baseball players from professional teams across America. For players, earning a spot in the Hall of Fame is a great accomplishment!

Baseball is one of New Yorkers' favorite sports. The Yankees and Mets are the home teams. Fans of both teams are very loyal. They fight about who's better!

Team sports are fun to watch. But New York has lots more to offer. Winter is the time for skiing and snowmobiling. Summer brings people to the beaches and lakes. Any time is great for hiking through the forests. New York has something for everyone!

The plaque gallery has information about famous baseball players.

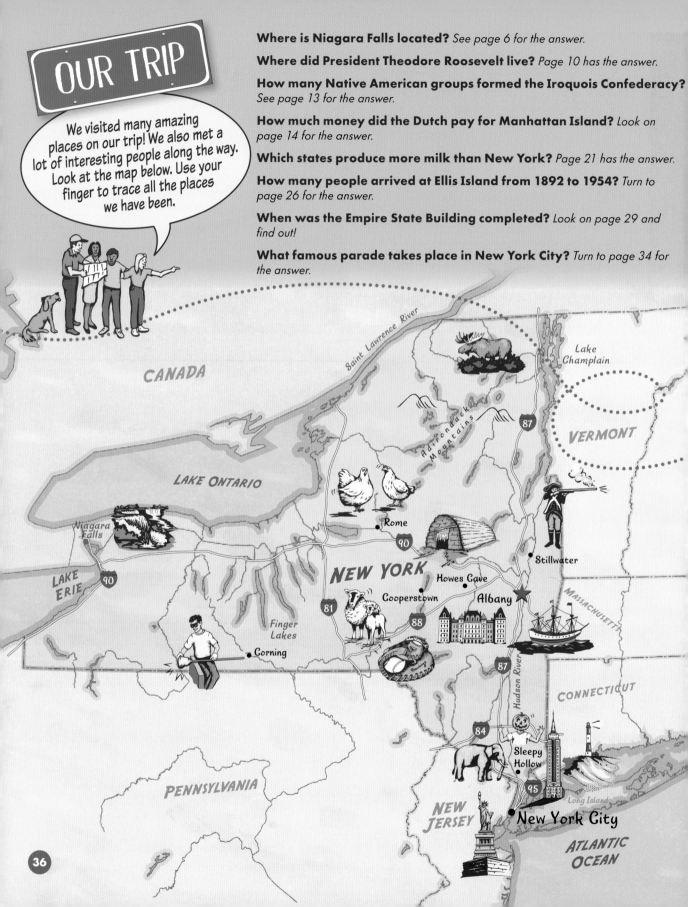

OUR TRIP

We visited many amazing places on our trip! We also met a lot of interesting people along the way. Look at the map below. Use your finger to trace all the places we have been.

Where is Niagara Falls located? *See page 6 for the answer.*

Where did President Theodore Roosevelt live? *Page 10 has the answer.*

How many Native American groups formed the Iroquois Confederacy? *See page 13 for the answer.*

How much money did the Dutch pay for Manhattan Island? *Look on page 14 for the answer.*

Which states produce more milk than New York? *Page 21 has the answer.*

How many people arrived at Ellis Island from 1892 to 1954? *Turn to page 26 for the answer.*

When was the Empire State Building completed? *Look on page 29 and find out!*

What famous parade takes place in New York City? *Turn to page 34 for the answer.*

CANADA

Saint Lawrence River

Lake Champlain

Adirondack Mountains

VERMONT

87

LAKE ONTARIO

Niagara Falls

Rome

90

NEW YORK

Howes Cave

Stillwater

LAKE ERIE

90

81

Finger Lakes

Cooperstown

88

Albany

MASSACHUSETTS

Corning

Hudson River

87

CONNECTICUT

84

Sleepy Hollow

95

Long Island

PENNSYLVANIA

NEW JERSEY

New York City

ATLANTIC OCEAN

State flag

State seal

STATE SYMBOLS

State animal: Beaver

State beverage: Milk

State bird: Bluebird

State fish: Brook trout

State flower: Rose

State fossil: *Eurypterus remipes*, an extinct relative of the sea scorpion and king crab

State fruit: Apple

State gem: Garnet

State insect: Ladybug

State muffin: Apple muffin

State shell: Bay scallop

State tree: Sugar maple

STATE SONG

"I LOVE NEW YORK"
Words and music by Steve Karmen

I love New York,
I love New York,
I love New York.
There isn't another like it.
No matter where you go.
And nobody can compare it.
It's win and place and show.
New York is special.
New York is diff'rent
'Cause there's no place else on earth
Quite like New York
And that's why
I love New York,
I love New York,
I love New York.

That was a great trip! We have traveled all over New York! There are a few places that we didn't have time for, though. Next time, we plan to visit Central Park in New York City. Central Park covers 1.32 square miles (3.42 sq km). It has a zoo, an ice skating rink, gardens, and more.

FAMOUS PEOPLE

Ball, Lucille (1911–1989), actress

Carter, Shawn Corey "Jay Z" (1969–), rapper

Combs, Sean "P. Diddy" (1971–), rapper and clothing designer

Cruise, Tom (1962–), actor

Gershwin, George (1898–1937), pianist and composer

Giuliani, Rudy (1944–), former mayor of New York

Gleason, Jackie (1916–1987), entertainer

Irving, Washington (1783–1859), author

Jordan, Michael (1963–), former basketball player

Klein, Calvin (1942–), fashion designer

Lombardi, Vince (1913–1970), former football player and football coach

Ray, Rachael (1968–), television show host, businesswoman, celebrity cook, author

Rockwell, Norman (1894–1978), painter and illustrator

Roosevelt, Eleanor (1884–1962), former First Lady and humanitarian

Roosevelt, Franklin D. (1882–1945), 32nd U.S. president

Roosevelt, Theodore (1858–1919), 26th U.S. president

Trump, Donald (1946–), businessman, 45th U.S. president

Truth, Sojourner (1797–1883), abolitionist and suffragist

Whitman, Walt (1819–1892), poet

Zuckerberg, Mark (1984–), computer programmer, Facebook creator

WORDS TO KNOW

boroughs (BUR-ohz) towns or sections that make up a large city

colonies (KOL-uh-neez) lands with ties to a mother country

diverse (DI-verse) differing from one another

Dutch (DUCH) having to do with the Netherlands

flax (FLAKS) a plant with fibers that can be made into thread

headquarters (HED-kwor-turz) a group's main office or meeting place

husks (HUHSKS) rough outer coverings

immigrants (IM-uh-gruhnts) people who leave their home country and move to another land

legends (LEJ-uhndz) old tales told to teach a lesson or explain something

muskets (MUHSS-kits) heavy guns used in the Revolutionary War

traditional (truh-DISH-uhn-uhl) following long-held customs

TO LEARN MORE

IN THE LIBRARY

Burgan, Michael. *Who Was Theodore Roosevelt?* New York, NY: Grosset & Dunlap, 2014.

Cunningham, Kevin. *The New York Colony.* New York, NY: Children's Press, 2012.

Demuth, Patricia Brennan. *What Was Ellis Island?* New York, NY: Grosset & Dunlap, 2014.

Stine, Megan. *Where Is Niagara Falls?* New York, NY: Grosset & Dunlap, 2015.

ON THE WEB

Visit our Web site for links about New York:

childsworld.com/links

Note to Parents, Teachers, and Librarians: We routinely verify our Web links to make sure they are safe and active sites. So encourage your readers to check them out!

PLACES TO VISIT OR CONTACT

New York State Museum

nysm.nysed.gov
222 Madison Avenue
Albany, NY 12230
518/474-5877

For more information about the history of New York

The Official Guide to New York City

nycgo.com
810 Seventh Ave, 3rd Floor
New York, NY 10019
212/484-1200

For more information about traveling in New York City

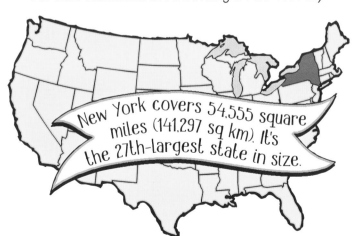

New York covers 54,555 square miles (141,297 sq km). It's the 27th-largest state in size.

INDEX

Bye, Empire State.
We had a great time.
We'll come back soon!